How To Get Out Of A Tough Spot

Ways to Win in Difficult Times

LOY B. SWEEZY, JR.

How to get out of a Tough Spot
Published by Loy Sweezy Ministries
P.O. Box 131
Austell, GA 30168

Printed in the United States of America

ISBN   987-0-9717546-2-1

www.loysweezy.com

Table of Contents

1

Recognize Where You Are

Before a person can get out of a tough spot, they must recognize where they are and what they need to do in order to get out. *"For I acknowledge my transgressions: and my sin is ever before me." (Psalms 51:3)* When a person recognizes what is going on with them, that means that they have a clear insight or understanding about what they are going through.

Recognizing where you are or what is going on with you, has to do with you examining yourself. Notice this scripture, *"Examine yourselves, whether ye be in the faith; prove your own selves, Know ye not your own selves, how that Jesus Christ is in you, except ye be reprobates?"*

(II Corinthians 13:5) When you examine your-self, you clearly understand right where you are and understand what you need to do in order to get out.

When you examine yourself, you will not blame others or shift the blame for where you are in life, you will own up to your responsibility to do what you have to do in order to get out of the tough spot.

When people can recognize, not only are they identifying the problem, but also in some cases, they recognize and are clearly aware of the contributing factors that are causing the problems.

> *And he said unto them, Take me up, and cast me forth into the sea; so shall the sea be calm unto you: for I know that for my sake this great tempest is upon you. Nevertheless, the men rowed hard to bring it to land; but they could not: for the sea wrought, and was tempestuous against them... So they took up Jonah, and cast him forth into the*

sea: and the sea ceased from her raging. (Jonah 1:12-13, 15)

I think it would be very important for me to say this before we continue; wrong association with people can produce hindrances and distractions in your life. One reason why people go through a lot of hell here on earth is that they have the wrong people around them.

The only way these mariners' lives could get better or back to normal was to throw Jonah overboard. This action indicates that there are some people and things in your life that you have to throw overbroad. Often times, you will not be able to get out of a tough spot until you get the problem out.

In the book of Jonah, God instructed Jonah to go unto Nineveh and preach repentance to the city. However, Jonah refused. He gets on a boat and heads into the opposite direction. (Jonah 1:1-3) One of the reasons for Jonah refusing to go to Nineveh is that he was dealing with an unforgiving attitude. He refused to forgive Nineveh of their brutal treatment toward other nations.

One of the main reasons why some people cannot get out of a tough spot is because they have not let go of a wrong that was done to them. You cannot hold onto mistreatment. You must give it over to God or it will give you over to a life full of heartaches, misery and pain. I strongly encourage you to read my book *Overcoming Bad Habits* to get a complete, in-depth understanding of Jonah's stages to change.

As we continue to study Jonah, he is a primary case of a person being arrogant about what he knew until his stubbornness caused him not to come out of his tough spot. The fact that he was able to recognize what was going on with him was good, which means that he was fully aware of his situation and had accepted the responsibility for what was occurring in his life and not willing to shift the blame towards someone else. However, the fact that he was not willing to obey God was not good. This is why: Not only did Jonah's flamboyant arrogance almost cost him his life, it also almost cost innocent lives around him.

After Jonah was thrown overboard at his request, the sea became calm and then a great fish swallowed up Jonah. (Jonah 1:17) Now Jonah goes through hell, hitting the bottom all because of his disobedience to obey and serve God. Hitting the bottom is when a person experiences a major crisis knocking him/her off balance, enabling the individual to look at things differently, taking a deep honest inventory of him/her, which ultimately causes this person to turn to God.

In most cases when a person hits rock bottom it is because they have disobeyed the word of God. It is the will of God for you to be above only and not beneath, that you enjoy life in abundance to full and have it running over. (Deuteronomy 28:13, Luke 6:38) If you are experiencing consistent setback, failures, and overwhelming complications that is a result of the devil trying to steal God's best from you.

> *The thief cometh not, but for to steal, and to kill, and to destroy: I am come that they might have life, and that they might have it more abundantly. (John 10:10)*

In addition, if you are disobedient to the call

of God or the will of God for your life, you will be the responsible party for the overwhelming complications in your life. Always remember that it is never God who punishes people; God loves you and He cares for you.

> *For I know the thoughts that I think toward you saith the LORD, thought of peace, and not of evil, to give you an expected end. (Jeremiah 29:11)*

It is your refusal to comply with the will of God, that opens up the door for catastrophes and overwhelming complications. *Yea, and all that live godly in Christ Jesus shall suffer persecution (II Timothy 3:12),* however, some persecutions that people suffer have nothing at all to do with God or the devil. It is the individual's blatant irresponsibility to obey the biblical precepts of the Word of God.

Notice this scripture,

> *BEHOLD, THE LORD'S hand is not shortened, that it cannot save; neither his ear heavy, that it cannot hear: But your iniquities have separated*

between you and your God, and your
sins have hid his face from you, that
he will not hear. (Isaiah 59:1-2)

These mariners on the boat lost almost everything trying to save Jonah, and the truth of the matter is that nothing could have saved Jonah but himself. Jonah needed to get right with God, meaning that Jonah would have had to repent and do exactly what God was asking him to do if things were going to get better.

For things to get better with you, you must get right with God to get out of a tough spot. *Come unto me* is the word of Jesus and He will give you rest (Matthew 11:28). However, this is something that you have to do. Come to Jesus. He is the way to get you out of a tough spot.

2

Turn to God

Let me give you a biblical example of the importance of turning to God during tough times. In II Chronicles 16:12-13, the Bible states, *"King Asa of Judah was diseased in his feet until his disease was exceedingly great. Yet in his disease, he sought not the Lord, but the physicians, and he died."* The reason for his death is that he did not turn to God.

God did not mind the doctors. In fact, God shared with the nation of Israel that because they did not walk in accordance to His commandments and statutes, their physicians were unable to recover the health of the people. *(Jeremiah 8:22)*

This is big: if you are going to truly overcome, you must turn to God when you are in a tough spot. Notice this scripture, *"God is our refuge and strength, a very present help in trouble." (Psalms 46:1)* During tough times you must not turn to your negative or addictive behaviors, you must turn to God and He will be the source that will get you out of the tough spot.

God works through the doctors and medications: *"A merry heart doeth good like a medicine." (Proverbs 17:22)* However, in this particular situation, the only one that could have healed this king was God. You are created by God and for God and there are certain things that can only be accomplished by God.

There is nothing wrong with taking appropriate medications prescribed by a trained, licensed physician. However, we are not to be dependent upon doctors to make us better. We are to be dependent totally on God.

> *And you shall serve the LORD your God, and he shall bless thy bread, and thy water; and I will take*

sickness away from the midst of thee.
(Exodus 23:25)

The reason for this king Asa's death was obvious; he did not turn to the Lord first. He sought the Lord after the fact. God does not want us to seek Him after we have made a mess. He wants us to seek Him before we make a mess.

"I will lift up mine eyes unto the hills, from whence cometh my help. My help cometh from the Lord, which made heaven and earth." (Psalms 121:1-2)

This King had a very prominent position, he was the King of Judah, which indicates that he was over the praise and worship of that particular tribe, yet in the midst of his dancing and shouting (and for some today, even speaking in tongues), and he died because he did not turn to God.

Notice this scripture,

Because they regard not the works of the LORD, nor the operations of his

*hands, he shall destroy them, and
not build them up. (Psalms 28:5)*

When a person refuses to incorporate God into their life and present situations, God can do nothing for them. When you disregard God, you disregard the operations of his hands to get involved in your situations; Therefore, by your own admission to not receive supernatural assistance from God, you now position yourself to be destroyed by whatever is coming against you.

3

Develop a Systematic Plan

When I speak of developing a system to help you get out of a tough spot, I am speaking in reference to setting up a plan of action on how you can overcome. In order to get out of a tough spot you must develop a system whereby you will be able to overcome your struggles. This is accomplished by coming up with a plan and working the plan.

Developing a systematic plan will help you set limits, goals and help you to evaluate your progress. The systematic plan will help you stay committed and focused on what you need to do.

One of the major tools to getting out of a tough spot is that you must set goals. Goal setting will help you with measuring the result of your out-come to determine if you are really achieving what you set out to do.

Goal setting helps you to write down a plan to where you will come up with new ideals and solutions that target your areas of improvements and it will provide a systematic approach on how you can improve in areas of your weaknesses.

Many people fail when it comes to setting goals. They know what they should do but for whatever reason they do not get around to doing it until the problem is detrimental or life threatening. You must develop a systematic plan and work the plan if the plan is going to work for you.

Scriptures says, *"But be ye doers of the word, and not hearers only, deceiving your own selves"*. *(James 1:22)* The book of James indicates that those who only receive the word are deceived, because it takes more to getting results in life than just knowing what to do.

You must do what you know if what you know is going to work for you. Therefore, developing a plan of action is good, but you must implement your plan into action to have effective results.

Developing a systematic plan is coming up

with new solutions. You will be replacing the bad things you do with good things. For instance, if you know that you have a problem with losing weight because of overeating, then you will need, for starters, to change your diet and exercise to lose weight.

In addition, it will not hurt for you to clean out your refrigerator of all unhealthy foods and replace them with foods that are low in fat. What did we just do? We came up with a new solution; we substituted or replaced one bad behavior for a good behavior.

If you have a problem with smoking, then you will need, for starters, to get rid of all the cigarettes. Next, you will need to avoid places that allow smoking, and then you will need to find some non-smoking friends, then read the Bible and pray. In addition, some may need to buy some nicoderm, which are patches designed to help stop smoking.

Again, what have we just done? We came up with a new solution; we have put in place preventive techniques to stop old behaviors and implemented new approaches to obtain the goal that is desired.

4

Do You Want to Get Out?

Often, church leaders and counselors become burned out and drained in a needless effort to get people to change. It does not matter how much they plead with people...the church leaders and counselors could sing until the cows come home; if a person does not want to change, then change will not occur. In fact, many times people's situations will get worse before they get better, making people ripe for change.

> *And, behold, a woman, which was diseased with an issue of blood twelve years, came behind him, and touched the hem of his garment: For she said within herself, If I may but touch his*

garment, I shall be whole. But Jesus turned him about, and when he saw her, he said, Daughter, be of good comfort; thy faith hath made thee whole. And the woman was made whole from that hour. (Matthew 9:20-22)

Every change starts with a decision to want to change. The woman with the issue of blood made a decision to turn to God. That is one of the main principles to getting out of a tough spot. Jesus said that I am the way (John 14:6); **we must make a decision to follow Jesus Christ if things are going to get better.**

The woman with the issue of blood made the decision, not someone else for her. Often times when people do things because others want them to, the results are not as lasting and effective as they would be if the person desiring to change because they know that they need to change.

One thing that stands out significantly with the woman with the issue of blood is that, *"She said within herself"*, this signifies that she kept on saying and saying until she achieved what she believed. She wanted to get out of what she was going through and she believed that she could receive her healing by touching Jesus. Because of her wanting to come out, she overcomes a tough spot.

This is very important to getting out of tough spots. **First; you need to know that you can achieve what you believe,** *"all thing are possible to him that believeth"* and this woman no doubt knew this by her attempt to get to Jesus. She knew that there lay within Jesus a supernatural ability to set her free. It is the same, my brother and sister, in your situation today. If you can just make a point of contact with Jesus, He will fix it for you.

Second; we see that this lady stayed with it, she did not quit even though she had to put forth a lot of effort and to work around the crowded conditions to get what she wanted; the scripture reference states that she pressed. The word *press* denotes *to bear down upon, push steadily against.* I like this definition, *to squeeze out all the juice.*

That is the key to getting out of a tough spot. You have to bear down, squeezing tightly and not letting go, you have to stay with it; you have to desire to recover, turn, change and come out of bondage so strongly that you are willing to soak up all the knowledge and input that is going to make you better.

If you are going to come out of a tough spot, you have to stay with what you know is right to do. Do not quit. You only fail when you stop trying. Although it may get tough, you have to be anchored and committed enough not to let anything distract, damage or deter you from what you are trying to accomplish. You can do it. The woman that had the issue of blood (Mark 5:25-29) stayed focused on what she believed.

The point I would like to make here is that it does not matter what you go through or what type of struggle you may presently be experiencing. You do not have to lose your mind; you do not have to accept defeat or failure as your final answer.

You can win, you can come out on top, and you can get out of tough spot, although it may appear that all of the surrounding evidence is pointing against you, you can win. Scripture says, *"Nay, in all these things we are more than conquerors through him that loved us."* *(Romans 8:37)*

Third, we see that this woman put forth a strong effort. If you are going to get out of a tough spot, you are going to have to put forth your best effort. This strong or best effort indicates this woman was willing to work through any struggles to get what she wanted. This caused her not to cave in, give up, or quit under pressure.

5

Why Some People Don't Overcome

The Bible says:

"*And Isaac prayed much to the Lord for his wife because she was unable to bear children, and the Lord granted his prayer, and Rebekah his wife became pregnant. [Two] children struggled together within her; and she said, if it is so [that the Lord has heard our prayer], why am I like this? And she went to inquire of the Lord. And the Lord said unto her, Two nations are in thy womb...*" (Genesis 25:21-23 NLT)

There was one thing that Isaac did that was very significant in this passage of scripture, he prayed, it was Isaac's prayer that enabled the hand of God to get involved with his situation; prayer has always been one of the main channels that God has provided for man to come into direct contact with Him.

There are four reasons that most people do not overcome during tough times. **One, they don't pray**, In Luke 18:1 *"And he spake a parable unto them to this end, that men ought always to pray, and not to faint."* People often give up and quit when they are not consistent in prayer. Every failure in life is because of a lack of prayer.

Prayer will keep you from doing the wrong thing. *"And said unto them, Why sleep ye? rise and pray, lest ye enter into temptation." (Luke 22:46)* People who do not pray consistently and effectively often get into trouble, they are more vulnerable to the attacks of demonic activity, and they are more likely susceptible to experiencing life threatening addictive chronic behaviors, because they are not praying.

Two, most people don't believe God, *"and*

all things, whatsoever ye shall ask in prayer, believing, ye shall receive." (Matthew 21:22) Prayer not believed is prayer not received. Do you believe? Many people when experiencing tough times will, after a period of time, begin to doubt and become weary about overcoming what they are going through. Many people give up, let go or even compromise their positions during tough times.

One of the keys to overcoming during tough times is that you must believe God; you must put your confidence in God and not in the doctor, lawyer, medicine or your own intellectualism. It is God who will help you and deliver you; it is God that will break the strong hold(s) and destroy the bad behavior(s); it is God that will give you the strength to overcome. The question is, do you believe it?

Three, most people don't ask in the name of Jesus, *"...that whatsoever ye shall ask of the father in my name, he may give it you." (John 15:16)* God will give to those who ask in the name of his son Jesus Christ, every prayer should be to the Father in the name of Jesus before or afterwards, everything must be done in the name of Jesus.

I remember while in Jamaica doing missionary work, my co-labourers and I went to one particular house. The woman asked for prayer for her son. She said that her son had been in ten fights at school. The year had just started and he was kicked out for the whole year. She said that her son was very, very angry (rage episodes) and began cutting on himself. He constantly refused to listen to anyone, and he was always getting in trouble. She said that she couldn't seem to do anything with him. We asked the woman to bring her son into the room.

This was the first time I ever saw anything like this. When the woman's son came into the room, I noticed that he took long jumps. When I looked down, I saw that he had a rope around his ankles about two inches thick. I noticed that his hands were tied together. This boy looked bad. You could see clearly that there was some demonic activity going on.

I remember lying hands on the young boy and speaking the Word of God over him. The young boy began to smile; his mother said that he had not smiled in a very, very long time.

The mother removed the rope from around his ankles. The boy began to cry and hugged his mother saying he was sorry.

God allowed me to witness at an early age that whatever has an individual bound can be broken, it is only the name of Jesus that is going to set him or her free. If you ask in the name of Jesus, God has promised to rescue you with what ever needs to be accomplished. (John 16:23)

One of the things to asking in the name of Jesus is that you must have things in order. You cannot be in sin, anger, un-forgiveness, or disobedience and expect God to get you out of a tough spot.

Four, most people are not active listeners, *"A wise man will hear, and will increase learning; and a man of understanding shall attain unto wise counsels." (Proverbs 1:5)* One of the reasons most people are not active listeners is because they are self absorbed in their own stuff (problems) which handicaps them from hearing (listening and obeying) positive instructional directions, we are instructed to be *"swift to hear, slow to speak"* (James 1:9)

6

Get Help

A sking someone to help you is one of the major ways to get out of a tough spot; there is an old saying that says: *"if you don't know, then ask somebody."* That is true because if you do not ask, in many cases people do not know that you have a need, especially in today's society. People are so busy with their own affairs of life, they do not have time to stop and question your personal struggles. Therefore, you have to make it known that you need help. There is nothing wrong with asking for help.

Scriptural References on Help

1. Call unto me, and I will answer thee, and show thee great and mighty things, which thou knowest not. (Jeremiah 33:3)

2. GOD IS our refuge and strength, a very present help in trouble. (Psalms 46:1)

3. I WILL lift up my eyes unto the hills, from whence cometh my help. My help cometh from the LORD, which made heaven and earth. (Psalms 121:1-2)

4. Our help is in the name of the LORD, who made heaven and earth. (Psalms 124:8)

5. So that we may boldly say, The Lord is my helper, and I will not fear what man shall do unto me. (Hebrews 13:6)

There are at least two reasons why some people do not ask for help: **1)** They are too ashamed and embarrassed to let people know that they are not doing so good; **2)** They do not want people in their so-called business. I call it pride and arrogance. When you know you need help, there are good people available who would love to help you. Do not refuse to get help;

accept their help.

In Luke 18:1-8, a woman kept asking a judge for help and finally the judge granted help to her. This woman was persistent and she looked in the right place. She went to the judge, and although the judge was very selfish, he had the resources that she needed (the authority to set her free) and she seized the moment by taking charge of the rights and privileges that were allotted her.

You have to be strong-willed about what you want to do and let nothing stop you from doing what is right. This woman went to the person who could make a difference in her life and the judge granted the request that she desired.

Notice this scripture,

And Peter answered him and said, Lord, if it be thou, bid me come unto thee on the water. And he said, Come. And when Peter was come down out of the ship, he walked on the water, to go to Jesus. But when he saw the wind boisterous, he was afraid; and beginning to sink, he cried, saying,

Lord, save me. And immediately Jesus stretched forth his hand, and caught him, and said unto him, O thou of little faith, wherefore didst thou doubt?" (Matthew 14:28-31)

There are some valuable lessons that we can learn from Peter. **First,** when Peter was in trouble (about to sink) he asked Jesus to help. This is a major oversight by many people attempting to get out of a tough spot; they do not ask for help. They will try to make it on their own, when help is all around them waiting and ready to be of support.

Second, Peter was not in the water long before asking Jesus for some assistance. Again, this is a major oversight by many people who struggle with getting out of a tough spot. They will wait until things are way out of order or control than ask for some help. When you first feel that you need some help that is when you need to ask.

The Bible says,

"Ye lust, and have not: ye kill, and desire to have, and cannot obtain:

ye fight and war, yet ye have not,
because ye ask not." (James 4:2)

When many people who are in tough spots realize they are incapable of getting out, then they run for help. You should ask for help anytime you feel that you are in need of help.

Third, We see that Peter just jumped into the water, Peter did not think about what he was getting himself into. When people make major decisions and do not think about what they are doing, this careless thinking does not turn out well. The majority of people who do this type of behavior will find themselves in a tough spot.

When a person makes quick, prompt, or impulsive decisions without counting the cost, again in most cases it will not work out well for the person in the end. It is always a good practice to think about what you are doing before you do it.

Scripture says,

"For which of you, intending to build
a tower, sitteth not down first, and

counteth the cost, whether he have sufficient to finish it." (Luke 14:28)

One of the advantages of thinking before you do something is that it will help keep you out of a tough spot. When you take your time to think or count the cost about what you are doing, you are eliminating the possibility of failure.

7

Obey Your
Positive Intuition

Obeying your positive intuition is crucial to coming or staying out of a tough spot. Many times when making a decision, people can sense what is right or what is wrong. People can sense that maybe they should not go to a certain place, do a certain thing, or hang around a certain person; nevertheless, many people do what they know or sense that they should not do. This, my brother and sister, will no doubt keep you in a tough spot.

The word **intuition** is derived from the Latin word *"intueri"* which means, *"to see within"*. Your intuition is more of an inner gut feeling, a perception of knowing something without the facts or credibility to explain it. Intuition is an ability to sense that something is right or wrong even though you do not have a clear understanding about it.

Every person has a human intuition, whether you are a Christian or not. Every person has the ability to perceive, discern, sense, or just get a feel for how things are going on around him or her. Some people use their intuition for good and others use it for bad.

Nevertheless, the more you develop in obeying those things that are right, loving, uplifting and promoting life, your intuition will keep you out of tough spots. However, when you are challenged with things that are negative, destructive, or maybe just not good for you, if you do those things you will find yourself eventually stuck in a tough spot.

I have some dictating software on my computer. This dictating software allows me to talk to my computer instead of typing. The only thing I have to do is just speak the words through a headset and my dictating software will type every single word that I say. However, before my computer could type what is said, I have to spend several minutes speaking into the headset so it could recognize my speech.

The speak recognition has to get accustomed to recognizing my voice. Once my voice was consistently recognized, the dictating software just took over automatically because it was familiar with my voice.

Your intuition is somewhat like the dictating software; **first,** you must get to a point to where you can recognize what your intuition is saying to you. **Second,** you need to do exactly what your intuition is communicating for you to do. I think it is extremely, extra important to say this. Your intuition will never tell you to do something that will physically harm or mentally abuse an individual.

Your intuition is a safety guide for you; your intuition is only concerned with the safety of your well-being. **Third,** the more you obey your intuition the easier it will become to hear and do what is being instructed to you by your intuition.

Your intuition is your conscience guidance. If you are a born again believer (Christian) who has trained your spirit in the word of God and prayer, your intuition would be your spirit witness.

Notice this scripture, *"I say the truth in Christ, I lie not, my conscience also bearing me witness in the Holy Ghost." (Romans 9:1)* Your spirit has an inward voice; this voice will prompt, stir, confirm and direct you to make proper decisions which results in keeping you out of tough spots.

The more Christians yield to the Holy Spirit the keener their intuition to perceive things from God's perspective will develop. Not obeying your intuition is unhealthy behavior; it is unhealthy because when you disregard your positive intuition you will set yourself up to enter into tough spots that are not designed for you. Your positive intuition is a safeguard to keep you in peace and rest.

Let me give you an example of not obeying your positive intuition. When I was working for a particular company, I decided to transfer to another department while I working in my current department. During the interviewing process with the department heads, I felt extremely uncomfortable, and I communicated this uncomfortable feeling to them, it was passed off as maybe not knowing each other well.

As I looked back over the situation, I realized that was not true at all; that uncomfortable feeling was my positive intuition indicating to me not to get involved.

My intuition about taking the job was not a fear but more of a maybe you should not do this. The whole time the interviewers were talking to me, I am sure they were sizing me up to assure the fact that I met the minimum requirement for the position. However, I was also observing them to determine, would I really be a fit for this particular department.

The department extended the opportunity for me to work for them, giving me a pay raise. The interesting thing about that is that I was not at all excited about taking the position, but the money sounded good. You must first be right or get in a right relationship with God for your money to have kingdom of God effectiveness. Your money has no kingdom of God sufficiency when you are out of the will of God.

The Bible talks about a man who had a lot of money (Luke 12:1-21); this man allowed his money (possessions) to govern his decision and not God. When this man died, he went to hell because he allowed his money to control his life and not God. When God is leading you, He will never lead you wrong.

Many people make decisions based on money. They will take jobs, positions, kiss up and do all sorts of things for fear of going broke, or for a desire to make it to the top. However, if you listen to God and do what He says, God will never allow you to go broke. God will keep you out of unnecessary struggles.

King David said it this way, *"I have been young and now am old, yet have I not seen the [uncompromisingly] righteous forsaken or their seed begging bread." (Psalms 37:25, AMP)* God will make sure that money comes to you and that you have more than enough; even some to give away.

God knows that we need money in the body of Christ. God does not want your money to control your decisions. God knows how to get money to the uncompromisingly righteous person. However, if your money controls you more than when God speaks to you about a decision, you will be unable to hear Him, because your mind is on your money and your money is on your mind.

On the first day of work in that particular department, when I walked through the door I knew that I did not need to be there; I could sense it in the air. I sensed that I needed to stay within my present department, just only working there.

People would ask me, how do you like the job and I would say things like oh, it's fine, as an attempt to not to speak any negativity about the department. Nevertheless, the more I worked on that job it was just an up hill struggle. I was moving too slowly, making a lot of mistakes, and was constantly being rushed to do more. I was trained by a minimum of twelve different people within a three-week period and all of them were saying something different, which complicated the whole process.

The whole time I was working, I was thinking to myself, why am I here? I do not really like this job. I did not like the job because I felt it was a lot of hustle and bustle. There were several days where I worked eight hours and did not even take a break. When leaving the department I was still behind on my work. In addition to confusion and competitive jealousy, I really just did not want to be a part of it.

I talked with one of the department heads about the struggle I was experiencing and I was encouraged to stay with it and told that things would get better. Things did not get better; in fact things became worse. I wanted to walk out the door several times.

Finally, after so much training I was exhausted. When one of the department heads suggested that I was not going to work out in that particular department, I thought to myself, boy what a relief that is. I had been contemplating letting the job go for weeks, and when the department head said that I felt a heavy burden lift off my shoulders.

Where the positive intuition comes into play is when I had feelings or perceived that this job was not good for me at the initial interviewing stage yet I still pursued it. My intuition was trying to keep me out of a tough spot, my intuition was trying to keep me from weeks of frustrations, staying up later at night, spending little time with my family, and regretting that I even became involved in the whole situation.

In Acts 27:10–11, the Bible states,

> *"And said unto them, Sir, I perceive that this voyage will be with hurt and much damage, not only of the lading and ship, but also of our lives. Nevertheless the centurion believed the master and the owner of the ship more than those things which were spoken by Paul."*

Your intuition can communicate to you how certain things are going to turn out even before those things occur. When the Apostle Paul was on a ship sailing for Rome, he had a perception; an intuition that the voyage was not going to be good. I think it is interesting to note that Paul did not say, *"The Lord spoke to me communicating that the voyage will be with hurt and much damage."* Paul just perceived; he had an inner prompting or sensibility that something was not going to be right ahead of them.

Notice what happened when the men on the

ship did not obey the Apostle Paul's intuition. These men kept sailing and ran directly into danger. They experienced a tough spot, and the storm became so bad until it started tearing up the ship. These men began throwing things overboard, and felt for sure that they were going to die.

The Bible states,

No one had eaten for a long time, finally, Paul called the crew together and said, "Men, you should have listened to me in the first place and not left Fair havens. You would have avoided all this injury and loss. But take courage! None of you will lose your lives, even though the ship will go down. (Acts 27:21–22, NLT)

Now the thing I want to say to you is that it did not have to be that bad for the folks on the ship, if they would have listened. In addition, when you do not listen to your intuition, whatever you are involved in will only take you down. These men's ship went down all because they refused to be sensitive to what was going on around them.

In II Chronicles 18:1-34, which I strongly recommend you reading in the New Living Translation of the Bible, King Ahab of Israel wanted to go to war against his enemy (Ramoth-gilead), but before he went into war, King Ahab asked Jehoshaphat, King of Judah to join him against Ramoth-gilead. King Jehoshaphat agreed to go into war with Ahab. However, before King Jehoshaphat would join in the war he wanted to know first what the Lord had to say about it.

> *"Will you join me in fighting against Ramoth-gilead?" Ahab asked. And Jehoshaphat replied, "Why, of course! You and I are brothers, and my troops are yours to command. We will certainly join you in battle." Then Jehoshaphat added, "But first let's find out what the LORD say." (II Chronicles 18:3-4)*

Seeking the Lord first and finding out in the beginning what God wants you to do is extremely important to staying out of tough spots. You need to know what does the Lord say about what you are going through. Whatever God has to say is always with the intent of you coming out on top or coming out the winner.

After King Jehoshaphat inquired to seek the Lord first, King Ahab had all of his prophets come in and they prophesied lies. King Ahab prophets said that it is all right to go into war. However, King Jehoshaphat began to use his intuition; he did not feel comfortable about King Ahab's prophets. Therefore, King Jehoshaphat, asked for a prophet to come; only this time one that was not a part of the king prophets,

King Jehoshaphat was concerned about his life; he needed spiritual guidance, and he did not want to go into a war and die prematurely. He wanted to know his outcome or at least gain a sense of was this the time for him to be going into war. He wanted to know if this was good judgment to support King Ahab in war. Notice this scripture,

> *Howbeit when he, the Spirit of Truth,*
> *is come, he will guide you into all*

truth; for he shall not speak of him-
self; but whatsoever he shall hear,
that shall he speak: and he will shew
you things to come. (John 16:13)

Sometimes to avoid tough spots you have to look beyond what you hear; you have to look beyond what sounds good or what sounds bad; you have to look beyond what has been done or has not been done, you need to listen to what is going on in the inside of you. What is your intuition or your gut feelings saying to you?

In most cases whatever your intuition is saying to you, that is what you need to do, especially when your intuition is full of the word of God and the Spirit of God. A Christian's Spirit (intuition) will always lead him/her in the right direction.

8

Get God Involved

Getting God involved in your tough spot is crucial to whether you will go over or go under. *"Call on me, and I will answer thee, and shew thee great and mighty things, which thou knowest not." (Jeremiah 33:3)* It is perfectly ok to call on God when you are in trouble. Many people think that they are misusing God or unworthy of God's help during tough times, especially when they know they are not living right.

Let me say this to you, **First**, God cannot be played, you cannot use, manipulate, or scheme God. **Second**, God's desire is that you ask him for help when you are in a tough spot, and when He answers you, his desire is that you continually follow him. Let us look at some biblical examples of people who called on God during tough times and God answered them and provided the victory for them.

People who God helped during Tough Times

1. **Jehoshaphat and all of Judah** called on the name of God and He helped them to victory over their enemies, who had come down to destroy them. (II Chronicles 20:1-30)

2. A great fish swallowed up **Jonah the prophet**, and God heard his cry and delivered him out of his affliction. (Jonah 2:1-10)

3. **The Children of Israel** cried due to their bondage to the Egyptians and God heard them and delivered them out of trouble. (Exodus 2:23-25)

4. The Psalmist **(David)** called on the name of the Lord and God heard him and lifted him up out of the pit of despair and destruction. (Psalm 40:1-3)

5. The **father of the demon-possessed boy**; the father asked Jesus to help him and Jesus healed the boy of his demonic possession. (Mark 9:14-29)

6. A **blind beggar** received his sight when he asked Jesus to have mercy on him and heal him. (Luke 18:35-43)

When you call on God during tough times God is able to heal, deliver, and set you free from fear, hurt, wrong, disappointments, buzzard behavior, and repeated offensives. God can get you out of a tight place or a tough spot. The thing to remember is that there is nothing too hard for God. All you need to do is humble yourself and get God involved in your situation. God knows how to get you out. God will communicate to you what you need to do and how you need to do it to accomplish your desired purpose.

You have to understand that you cannot and will not overcome certain habits with self will power. **Self will power is not the answer**; you must have a dependence on God. If you have not submitted your negative behaviors to God in times of weakness, you will give in and participate in the sin. God cannot do anything for you until you ask him to get involved.

Prayer will allow God to supernaturally get involved in your life, what I mean by supernatural is God exceeding beyond human ability, (Ephesians 3:20). I would strongly recommend you to read my book, *Breaking Free* to learn more about how prayer can commission the hand of God to work on your behalf.

The supernatural power of God is revealed in Mark 9:14-29. A man brought his son to Jesus' disciple to cast out a demon that they could not. Jesus' response to the situation was *"this kind can only come by prayer and fasting."* There are certain kinds of things (tough spots) in life that must be addressed only spiritually or supernaturally through prayer and fasting. This boy did not have a mental problem; he had a spiritual problem, which began when he was a child.

This indicates that you cannot allow things to go unchecked for a long period. If you allow problems to persist, the situation will not get better but worse. This is where we get the word stronghold (yoke), which is something that has a forceful grip on the mind, body, or spirit of an individual. The key to overcoming strong-holds is to get consumed with the word of God and to commit oneself to prayer and fasting.

Many people often make commitments and vows only to break them as soon as they make them. I believe one reason is that God was not asked to get involved. God will not do anything without your permission. The word **permit** means *to give one's consent or authorization to do something.* The important thing about permitting is that you allow access to be granted in your life.

Note this scripture, *"Thus saith the LORD, the Holy One of Israel, and his Maker, Ask me of things to come concerning my sons, and concerning the work of my hands command ye me."* Isaiah 45:11) In defining the Hebrew word for **command**, it means to *give legal right to by appointing or assigning.* This means that God cannot get involved into your situation without you appointing him.

For God to get involved in getting you out of a tough spot without your approval would be in violation of the word of God. *"Behold, I stand at the door, and knock; if any man hear my voice, and*

*open the door, I will come in to him, and will sup
with him, and he with me." (Revelations 3:20)*

This scripture indicates that Jesus cannot
enter into anyone's life without them opening
the door of their heart for Him to come in. If one
does not open the door of their heart, giving Jesus
authorization, and appointing him to work on their
behalf, Jesus will be in violation to enter into one's
life because he was not permitted to do so. You
have to give God permission to help you.

In Genesis 25:21-26, Isaac's wife, Rebekah
contrary to the woman with the issue of blood,
Rebekah sought God first about the complications she was having in her stomach. God
immediately communicated to her (Rebekah)
that she was birthing twins and these twins
would be two rival nations that would be at
opposition against one another, explaining the
reason for her stomach complications.

Now think about this for a moment; if
Rebekah would have sought a relative, friend
or maybe a doctor about her complications before
she consulted God, she could have possibly been
communicated some bad news or incorrect advice.
She could have been improperly diagnosis as

having experienced a miscarriage, or needing to take medication for pain relief.

Rebekah did not need any advice from others at that time. What she needed was a word from God, so that she could know the truth concerning her struggling. This truth would cause her not to lose time, money and energy unnecessarily on things she should not be doing.

9

God Can Locate You

*A*gain, Jesse made seven of his sons
to pass before Samuel. And Samuel
said unto Jesse, The LORD hath not
chosen these. And Samuel said unto
Jesse, Are here all thy children? And he
said, There remaineth yet the youngest,
and behold, he keepeth the sheep. And
Samuel said unto Jesse, Send and fetch
him: for we will not sit down till he come
hither. And he sent, and brought him in.
Now he was ruddy, and withal of a beau-
tiful countenance, and goodly to look to.
And the LORD said, Arise, anoint him:
for this is he. (I Samuel 16:10-12)

God located David out in the field: The prophet Samuel was sent by God to go to Jesse of Bethlehem to anoint a king from his sons. Jesse presented seven sons to Samuel and the LORD chose none of them. Samuel the prophet asked if there were any more sons, so Jesse sent for his youngest son David who was out in the field.

When David came into the house, the prophet Samuel anointed David to be King over Israel. Although David was the last one to be called to stand before the prophet, God worked through (bypassed) all of David's brothers and located David in the field tending to the sheep.

The point that I want to make is; **just because people are ahead of you or appear to be above you does not mean that they are better than you are**. God created you to be the best; therefore, it is important for you not to become frustrated about what is going on in your life right now because where you are presently is not where you are going to be permanently.

The key to God locating you is that you remain faithful, dedicated and committed to doing what you are called to do. If you do not stop trying and if you stay committed to be faithful and walk in integrity right where you are, opportunities will come available for you to make a difference.

Often times breakthroughs, recoveries, or blessings comes through you just staying with it; you just have to keep chipping away at the problem, challenge, struggle, or whatever you are trying to overcome. Just like George Washington, who chopped down the cherry tree, if you maintain steadfastness or perseverance whatever you are challenged with will break; it will come down and you will overcome. All problems can be solved and every challenge has a solution.

An Arabian proverb quotes that perseverance is *"the greatest of all teachers." (P.433)* This is important, when things do not look good, feel good, or even sound good, you have to stay faithfully committed to doing what you do and your time will come. Oftentimes people want to experience the results of instant satisfaction or success, but they fail to realize that opportunity comes with integrity, perseverance, hard work, and accountability.

Then the Lord said to me, "Write my answer in large, clear letters on a tablet, so that a runner can read it and tell everyone else. But these things I plan won't happen right away. Slowly, steadily, surely, the time approaches when the vision will be fulfilled. If it seems slow, wait patiently, for it will surely take place. It will not be delayed." (Habakkuk 2:2-3, NLT)

Again, God can locate you right where you are; you just need to be patient and faithfully committed where you are. The Bible says, *"And all these blessings shall come on thee, and overtake thee, if thou shalt hearken unto the voice of the LORD thy God." (Deuteronomy 28:2)* God knows how to locate you and be a blessing to you right where you are. You just need to be consistently optimistic in doing all you know you can do and then God will come help, to do what you cannot do.

Although there may be delays, set backs, or even hindrances to what you are trying to accomplish, you have to keep a right attitude and be respectful to all people and your time will come. Let us look at some biblical people who were faithful and committed and opportunity came knocking.

Opportunity came knocking to:

1. Queen Esther - She became the queen in place of queen Vashti; this replacement allowed queen Esther to be in a position to be a lifesaver and restorer when a commandment came forth to kill her people, the Jews. A nation was saved from death because of Queen Esther making a difference. (Esther 2:17, 4:14)

2. Moses – He was minding his own business, tending his father-in-law's sheep on the back side of the wilderness and God came to him and spoke to him through a burning bush, indicating to Moses that He (God) had come to deliver the Children of Israel out of the Egyptian Bondage and He (God) would use Moses to be the leader over the people. (Exodus 3:1-10)

3. The Apostle Peter – He was on the rooftop of his house praying and God came to him in a trance and communicated to him that three men would come looking for him and he was not to hesitate to go with them not doubting anything (Acts 10:9-23)

4. The First Disciples – Jesus came to each disciple specifically, calling them by name to follow him and to be his disciples and they (Simon surname Peter and his brother Andrew, James and his brother John) followed him. (Mark 1:14-19)

10

The Rabbit versus The Turtle

I remember in elementary school when my teacher taught us the story of the rabbit and the turtle *(hare and tortoise)* that ran in a race. Although the rabbit appeared to be stronger, faster and even smarter than the turtle, the rabbit lost the race because the turtle had contentment, commitment, discipline and determination not to give up.

The Bible states, *"...But he that shall endure unto the end, the same shall be saved." (Mark 13:13)* When you can learn to stand firm, trusting in God and his word, you will accomplish the thing you so desire, because it is God's desire to give you the desires of your heart. (Luke 12:32, Psalms 37:4)

The word **endure** according to the Expanded Vine's Expository Dictionary of New Testament Words, is *hupomeno* or *hoop-om-en'-o* which denotes *to abide under or to bear up courageously.* It also carries with it the connotation of *patiently waiting.* To endure is to rise or bear up under intense pressure. You will not be intimidated, distracted, or manipulated by what you know or don't know, you will only believe what you are trying to accomplish and you will be consistent in waiting to get your promises.

It was the turtle's consistence that allowed him to complete and win the race. The turtle was constantly the same during the race and was not moved by intimidation, distraction or manipulation by the rabbit getting so far ahead. The turtle stayed within his means, and although he was moving slow, the turtle understood that he was making progress, little progress is better than no progress at all; stay active and keep your mindset fixed on moving forward.

In junior high school, I was a member of the track and field team; my main event was the mile race. My coach would often remind the team runners to watch out for the opponent team's rabbit. The rabbit was a runner from the opposing team whose specific job was to make you burn out, and lose the race.

The rabbit initially would have all the attention on him because he would take off so fast at the beginning of the race, but that was only a manipulation or distraction to make you speed up, only to burn out and lose the race. The rabbit would very seldom finish the race. One reason is that the rabbit was set in place to help its other teams mates win. The rabbit could be another form of a guinea pig or a decoy. The rabbit sole purpose is to set you up real pretty for a big fall.

The interesting thing about the turtle in the race is that he did not fall for any of the rabbit's chauvinistic facade behaviors. The turtle stayed within the perimeters of what it could do and the turtle did what it knew it could do and did it well and did not allow all the outside or external situations to influence him to do something that he could not or did not want to do.

This is going to be one of your main tools to

you getting out of a tough spot. You will have to have determination, contentment and commitment to endure through the tough times. Stay in your lane; do not get upset or jealous because of what you see other people doing. You have to know who you are and what you can do and be content and committed to doing your best. You do your best and let God do the rest.

The turtle stayed the course and won the race. There is another reason for the turtle winning the race. He **never looked back**. Another main tool in getting out of a tough spot is that you cannot look back.

The only time you need to look back is when you are reflecting on the goodness that God has done for you in times past. Other than that, you should never look back, especially when you become negative, sad, depressed or when you begin to reject yourself or look down on yourself.

Despite everything negative in life that has happened to you, you have to keep moving on and not let it get you down. On the other hand, the rabbit, kept looking back. The rabbit wanted to see how far ahead he was in front of the turtle. The rabbit was far ahead of the turtle until he decided to take a nap and while the rabbit slept, the turtle passed by the rabbit and won the race.

11

Stay Away from Negative Activity

In order for you to come out of a tough spot, you will have to avoid places, things and people that cause you to do negative activities. Scriptures says, *"Wherefore come out from among them, and be ye separate, saith the Lord, and touch not the unclean thing; and I will receive you." (II Corinthians 6:17)* Staying away from negative associations is structured to keep you out of negative repeated behaviors.

Staying away from negative activities is sometimes you changing your friends, places, and things that can easily get you back into tough spots. Staying away from negativity will help you cut down on the unnecessary conflicts and keep you out of trouble.

The Bibles says, *"A prudent man foreseeth the evil, and hideth himself; but the simple pass on, and are punished." (Proverbs 27:12)* Avoidance will keep you out of unsafe environments and help you to avoid negative situations. By staying away from negative activities, you will not have to deal with the confusion and the pressure that is associated with doing wrong.

> *I have refrained my feet from every evil way, that I might keep thy word. (Psalms 119:101)*

One of the best ways to stay out of a tough spot is to live holy. Living holy is living right. Living right is following God's word; it is becoming one with God and His word (the Bible). God has called every born-again believer to live holy. There is nothing wrong with living holy.

Scripture declares, *"Be you holy because God is holy."* One of the ways you get close to God is to stop deliberately sinning, and to consistently live holy and pure in mind, body and spirit.

Again, one of the best ways to stay out of a

tough spot is to stay free of demonic activity in your life. Keep your heart right by living holy and staying away from all activities that are associated with sin.

> *"Do not let any part of your body become a tool of wickedness, to be used for sinning. Instead, give yourselves completely to God since you have been given new life. And use your whole body as a tool to do what is right for the glory of God."* (Romans 6:13, NLT)

Sin will bring evil spirits into your life attempting to destroy everything about you. The devil's purpose is to rob the body of Christ of its identity (John 10:10); if the body of Christ does not know who they are; the body of Christ will never be free to achieve God's best.

12

Don't Look Back

An example of not looking back was when I was at home one night watching a college football game. A defensive back intercepted the ball and ran about sixty yards, and right when he was close to the touchdown line he kept looking back; the opposing team player caught up and grabbed him by the back of his jersey and pulled him down at the one-yard line.

The point is this, in life, many people keep looking back and because they keep looking back, it prevents them from crossing over or entering into their greatness. Many times, we are right at the point of entering into what we desire, but because we turn back or look back, we come up short.

In order to get out of a tough spot you have to get it settled that I am going on, no more looking back, or turning back. I forgive myself and I forgive any and everybody who has done me wrong. You have to be committed not to allow what others think, feel, say or do to you, stop you from doing what God said you could do.

Let us take an automobile for instances; every automobile has windows and mirrors attached to it. The windows and mirrors that I have chosen to select are as follows; the front window, the back window, the rearview mirror, and the side mirror. When you are going forward, the **front window** is design specifically to get you to your destination. In addition, not only are you focused on where you are heading (destination) but you have a clear and wide view of what is in front of you because you are looking ahead.

When you are going forward and you decide for whatever reason to turn around, and look through the **back window,** it then becomes impossible for you to stay focused on where you are heading. The reality is that you do not even know where you are headed because you are turned around. You have no focus of what is before you; you will be like a wreck going somewhere to happen. When you look back, remember, you lose sight of where you are going. It was once stated, *"If you don't know where you are headed then any road will get you there."*

When you look through your **rearview mirror** you are not literally turning a round looking back, but it is as though you were looking back because you have decided to see a small glimpse of what is going on behind you. A good driver will never spend the majority of his or her time looking in the rearview mirror; the rearview mirror is only designed to take a glimpse at what is behind you for the moment.

The **side mirror** is designed for you to be aware of what is going on around you. However, you cannot be so focused on what is going on around you until you lose sight of what is ahead of you. You only need to look in the side mirror to reflect on what is happening around you, and then you put your eyes forward and keep your attention on where you are going.

One of the purposes for windows and mirrors being attached to a car is so that you can safely arrive at your destination. Getting out of a tough spot has a very similar approach. If you want to arrive at your destination in life you will need to stay focused on the things that you want to do.

In addition, you should only look back on your life to reflect on good things or things that you can learn or grow from; however, you will have to make it a point that you will not dwell on past disappointments. Dwelling on past disappointments will cause you to criticize yourself to the point of you becoming addicted to chaos and confusing been ongoing in your life, some people are addicted to experiencing trouble.

The Bible says that you shall be above only and not beneath, and that God will make you the head and not the tail. (Deuteronomy 28:13) The Bible says that God will increase you more and more, you and your children. (Psalms 115:14) After reading those scriptures, I am fully persuaded that God's will for your life is that you excel, get out of a tough spot, and avoid things that are stunting maximization in your life.

Again, the Bible says that God will make you the head; the head means that you are the man or woman in charge. Therefore, you cannot look at where you are and determine where you are going to continually be.

When you go through difficult situations, you must understand two things. One, God is going to get you out, and two, where you are is not where you are going to permanently remain.

Biblical Examples of God's Help during Tough Times

1. Daniel was put in a den of lions but he did not stay in the den because God delivered him out of the den of lions. Daniel had full confidence that God would not allow him to be eaten by the lions. However, those that accused Daniel of doing wrong for praying to his God three times a day, were thrown into the den of lions and the lions ate them to pieces. (Daniel 6:10-24)

2. The Hebrew boys were thrown into the fiery furnace because they refused to worship the king's idol that he had set up. However, they did not stay in the fiery furnace because God delivered them out and there was no harm

nor hurt on them when they came out of the fire. However, all their accusers were thrown into the fiery furnace, and burned to death. (Daniel 3:1-30)

3. Joseph was put in a pit, sold into slavery, and thrown into prison but he did not stay, he came out of the pit, he came out of slavery, he came out of prison and God elevated him to the second highest position in all the land of Egypt. God can get you out of whatever you are stuck in. (Genesis 37:23-28, 39:20-23, 41:37-45)

The key to Daniel, Hebrew Boys and Joseph coming out of everything they when through was the blessing of God upon their life. When you have the blessing of God, you have the favor of God upon your life, it does not matter how bad things look, God is going to bring you out and take you into your wealthy place.

Thou hast caused men to ride over our heads; we went through fire and through water: but thou broughtest us out into a wealthy place, (Psalms 66:12)

The Bible indicates in the book of Matthew 6:33, *"Seek ye first the Kingdom of God and his righteousness; and all these things shall be added unto you."* Total restoration and recovery begins and ends with God. You were created by God and for God and there are certain things in life that can not and will not be obtainable until you seek God and discover what He wants you to do.

Seeking the kingdom of God is discovering God's way of doing things. God's way is always the right way. Our own ways often led us astray and down wrong paths. Note this scripture, *"There is a way that seemeth right unto a man, but the end thereof are the ways of death." (Proverbs 16:25)*

13

Don't Get Bitter,
but Get Better

Therefore they did set over them taskmasters to afflict them with their burdens. And they built for Pharaoh treasures cities, Pithom and Raamses. But the more they afflicted them, the more they multiplied and grew. And they were grieved because of the children of Israel. (Exodus 1:11-12)

The children of Israel became stronger and stronger through the hardship placed on them by the Egyptians. The children of Israel multiplied and grew under the pressure of trouble. *"Many are the afflictions of the righteous: but the LORD delivereth him out of them all. (Psalms 34:19)* In the midst of difficulties, mistreatments, mental and physical abuse, the children of Israel believed God.

They knew that God had a plan and a purpose for their lives. They knew that although they where going through afflictions it was a temporary process, because God was going to bring them out of bondage. My brother and sister, God will do the same for you, in the center of discombobulation and hard times God will give you the knowledge, wisdom and strength to come out of your tough spot.

In life, you will experience tough spots, but that does not mean that you pack your bags and leave or quit, ignoring what God instructed you to do. No, you stay in there and believe that your situation will get better. Watch what God can do to make your situation make you better.

There is a story about a man who had a donkey; the man's donkey would never do what he asked it to do. Rather than shooting the donkey, the man decided to put the donkey in a very deep pit where people throw their trash, thinking that the donkey would just suffocate and die.

When people began to throw their trash in the pit, the donkey shook off the trash and stepped on it. This method of the donkey continued many days. Every time someone threw his/her trash in the pit, the donkey would shake it off and step on it.

Finally, with enough shaking it off and stepping on it, the donkey was able to become so high to the point that he was able to walk right out of the mess. The point is this: you can walk out of your tough spot; you can get out of whatever is trying to keep your down. You can get up from a fall, you can overcome a setback, you can win when others seem to think it is impossible, you can do all things through Christ. (Philippians 4:13)

Scriptures References on Getting Up

1. ARISE, SHINE, for thy light is come and the glory of the LORD is risen upon thee. (Isaiah 60:1)

2. LET GOD arise, let his enemies be scattered: let them also that hate him flee before him. (Psalms 68:1)

3. Rejoice not against me, O mine enemy: when I fall, I shall arise; when I sit in darkness, the LORD shall be a light unto me. (Micah 7:8)

4. For a just man falleth seven times, and riseth up again: but the wicked shall fall into mischief. (Proverbs 24:16)

5. Restore unto me the joy of salvation; and uphold me with thy free spirit. (Psalms 51:12)

6. I WAITED patiently for the LORD; and he inclined unto me, and heard my cry. He brought me up also out of an horrible pit, out of the miry clay, and set my feet upon a rock, and established my goings. (Psalms 40:1-2)

And Joseph said unto his brethren, Come near to me, I pray you. And they came near. And he said, I am Joseph your brother, whom ye sold into Egypt. Now therefore be not grieved, nor angry with yourselves, that ye sold me hither; for God did send me before you to preserve life. (Genesis 45:4-5)

One of the ways to overcome bitterness is that you cannot allow where you are presently to determine where you will be permanently. Joseph could have become stuck right there in the midst of his past hurts.

He could have lost his mind over the fact that his own brothers disliked him so much that they sold him into slavery at the age of seventeen (17) and lied to their father about it.

Nevertheless, Joseph refused to allow his past traumas to set him back. Joseph did not get bitter, but he became better. Joseph stayed focused and kept his eyes on what God was doing in his life, which brought him from the pit to the palace.

Again, one of the things that made Joseph so great is that he never became bitter. He just used everything he went through to make him better. Do not get bitter, get better. Joseph, very easily, could have become angry with God.

Joseph could have become angry with his father for showing him so much favoritism over his brothers. Joseph's father's favoritism for Joseph enabled Joseph's brothers to be jealous, and provoked them to do the evil that they did to Joseph. (Genesis 37:3-4)

Joseph could have become bitter at Potiphar's wife, who lied on him, and Joseph could have become bitter at Potiphar sentencing Joseph to be imprisoned (Genesis 39:7-20) However, Joseph did not do evil for evil nor did he become bitter at people that did him wrong.

He shook it off, stepped on it and stepped up. That is what you and I have to do...we have to shake off negative thoughts, past hurts, evil desires, and wrong behaviors, and use negativity and opposition as an opportunity for advancement.

ABOUT THE AUTHOR

Loy B. Sweezy, Jr. is a graduate of East Coast Bible College in Charlotte, North Carolina, with a Bachelor of Science Degree. While at East Coast Bible College, he did missionary work in India, Germany and Jamaica. He is a graduate of the School of Theology in Cleveland, Tennessee, with a Master's Degree. He is currently working on a Doctoral Degree at Oral Roberts University in Tulsa, Oklahoma.

He has worked as a chaplain in pastoral care and counseling department for both Carolina Medical Center in Charlotte, North Carolina and Princeton/Montclair Hospital in Birmingham, Alabama. He currently works as a mental health and substance abuse counselor for Ridgeview Institute located in Smyrna, Georgia.

God has called Loy B. Sweezy, Jr. to teach the Word of Faith and to encourage and inspire people who are sick, afflicted, hurting and seem to be in a hopeless situation; to change their thinking and circumstances by the knowledge and practice of the Word of God, enabling them to be all they can be in God and experience a life full of victorious living. "For with God nothing is ever impossible and no word from God shall be without power or impossible of fulfillment." (Luke 1:37, Amp)

Other Books Available
By Loy B. Sweezy, Jr.

Breaking Free
Overcoming Bad Habits

You can respond to the author by writing to:

Loy Sweezy Ministries

P.O. Box 131

Austell, Ga 30168

You can order this book and other materials
by calling toll-free 1-866-873-6330

For more information about Loy Sweezy,
please visit at **www.loysweezy.com**

Note

Note

Note

www.ingramcontent.com/pod-product-compliance
Lightning Source LLC
Chambersburg PA
CBHW031521040426
42445CB00009B/335